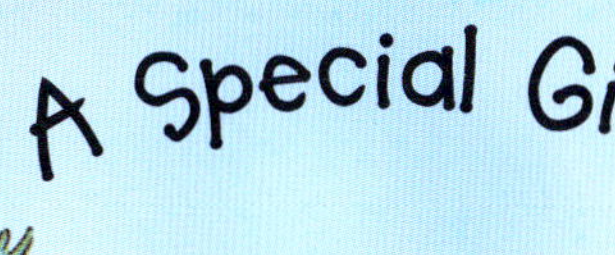

For

From

Date

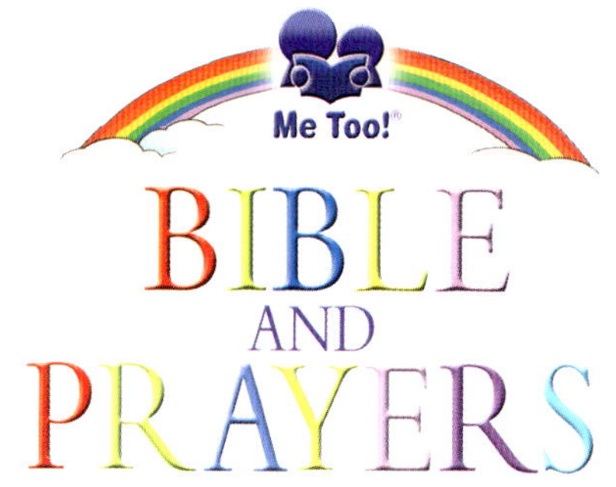

BIBLE AND PRAYERS

Stories retold by
Mary Hollingsworth

Illustrations by
Stephanie McFetridge Britt

Contents

New Testament Stories 85

OLD TESTAMENT

STORIES

God Made the World

God made the world. And He made everything in it. He made the sun and moon. He made seas and dry land. He made plants. He made fish, birds, and animals. Then He made man and woman.

God was happy with what He had made.

GENESIS 1:1–25

Point to something that God made.

All things bright and
beautiful,
All creatures great and small,
All things wise and wonderful,
The Lord God made them all.

He gave us eyes to see them,
And lips that we might tell
How great is God Almighty,
Who has made all things well!

Carl Frances Alexander

Adam and Eve

The man and woman God made were named Adam and Eve. They lived in a beautiful garden called Eden. They took care of the garden for God. The garden was full of wonderful fruit trees and plants. God let Adam name all the animals.

Adam and Eve were very happy in Eden.

GENESIS 1:26 – 2:25

Can you find the lion in the picture?

Dear Father,
Hear and bless
Thy beasts and singing birds.
And guard with tenderness
Small things that have no words.

Unknown

Noah's Big Boat

People on earth had become bad. Noah was the only good man. God decided to flood the earth with water. So, He told Noah to build a big boat to save his family. God sent two of each animal for Noah to put on the boat.

It rained for 40 days and nights. Water covered everything. But everyone on the big boat was safe and dry.

GENESIS 6:9 – 8:22

Where is Noah in the picture?

When the weather is wet,
We must not fret.
When the weather is cold,
We must not scold.
When the weather is warm,
We must not storm…
Be thankful together,
Whatever the weather.

Unknown

Joseph's Special Coat

Jacob had 12 sons, and Joseph was his favourite. Jacob gave Joseph a special coat. Then Joseph's brothers became angry. They sold Joseph to some men going to Egypt.

Joseph became a slave for one of the king's workers. And that's just where God wanted him to be.

GENESIS 37, 39:1–6

What colours are in Joseph's coat?

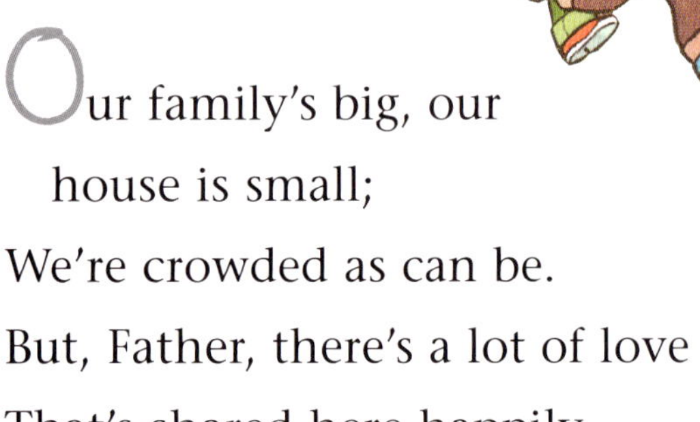

Our family's big, our
  house is small;
We're crowded as can be.
But, Father, there's a lot of love
That's shared here happily.

I love my mum and daddy, too;
They keep me safe each day.
But thanks for brothers and sisters,
  Lord;
They have more time to play.

Mary Hollingsworth

Baby Moses

When Moses was a baby, his mother had to hide him from the mean king of Egypt. She made a baby boat for him. She hid Moses in the boat in the Nile River.

The king's daughter found Moses and adopted him. Moses grew up in the king's own house, just as God had planned.

EXODUS 1:22 – 2:10

Who found baby Moses in the river?

Thank You for my parents, Lord,
and all the fun we've had.
There's no time I love better
than with my mum and dad.

Help me, Lord, to always know
the many ways they care.
For toys and snacks and big bear hugs
and always being there.

When I grow up, I want to be
just like my parents, too.
Because they make me feel so great
and love me just like You.

Beth Burt

A Burning Bush

When Moses was older he saw a burning bush. But the bush did not burn up. Moses went toward the bush, and God's voice spoke from the bush. "Moses, do not come closer. Take off your shoes. You are on holy ground."

Then God asked Moses to rescue His people from Egypt.

EXODUS 3:1–20

Dear God, you are the God who is,
the one whose name is I Am.

Mary Joslin

Leaving Egypt

Moses and his brother Aaron went to see the king of Egypt. They said, "God wants you to let His people leave Egypt." The king said, "No." So, God made ten terrible things happen to Egypt.

Finally, the king let God's people go. And Moses led them out of Egypt so they wouldn't be slaves.

EXODUS 7:10 – 12:33, 14:30–31

Can you point to the king of Egypt?

Lord, with Your praise we drop off
to sleep.
Carry us through the night,
Make us fresh for the morning.
Hallelujah for the day!
And blessing for the night!

from a Ghanaian fisherman's prayer

God's Ten Laws

After God's people left Egypt, God gave them ten laws. He wanted them to obey these laws. He wrote the laws on big stones and gave the stones to Moses.

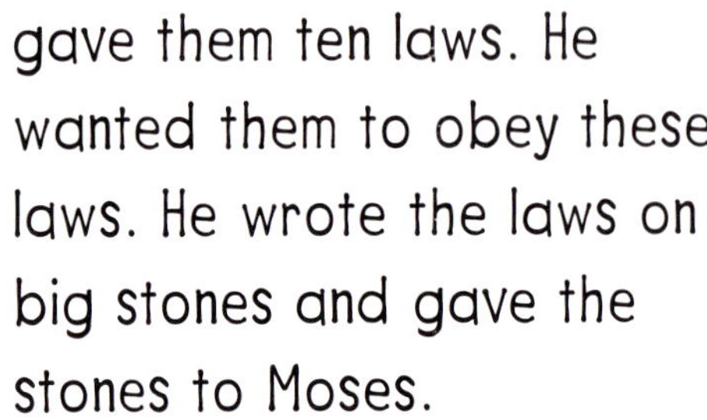

These ten laws helped God's people to be pure and holy. The laws are called the Ten Commandments.

EXODUS 20:1–17, 24:12–14, 32:15–16

What is Moses holding?

Two little eyes to look to God;
Two little ears to hear His word;
Two little feet to walk in His ways;
Two little lips to sing His praise;
Two little hands to do His will;
And one little heart to love Him still.

Traditional

Jericho's Walls Fall Down

God wanted the Israelites to capture the city of Jericho. Now, Jericho had big, tall walls around it. So, God had the people march around the city once a day for six days. On the seventh day, He had them go around seven times. Then He had them blow their horns and shout. And the walls of Jericho fell down.

The Israelites captured the city because they obeyed God.

JOSHUA 6:1–17, 20

When did the walls fall down?

Dear God,

Thank you that nothing is too difficult for you.

Nothing can stand in the way of what you want.

Unknown

Samson and Delilah

Samson was the strongest man who ever lived. What made him strong was a secret. Delilah was the woman Samson loved. She tricked him, and he told her his long hair was the secret.

Delilah had Samson's hair cut off while he slept. Then Samson was weak, and his enemies captured him.

JUDGES 16:4–22

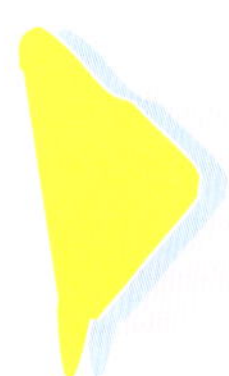

Do you know a secret?
Should you tell it?

If I were a butterfly,
I'd thank You, Lord, for giving me
wings,
And if I were a robin in a tree,
I'd thank You, Lord, that I could
sing,
And if I were a fish in the sea,
I'd wiggle my tail, and I'd giggle
with glee,
But I just thank You, Father,
for making me *me*.

Brian Howard

Ruth and Naomi

Ruth married Naomi's son. But the son died. Then Ruth and Naomi moved to a country called Judah. Naomi's cousin Boaz lived there. He had a big wheat field. Boaz let Ruth pick up grain from his field to feed Naomi.

Boaz soon married Ruth. And they had a son named Obed. Naomi took care of Obed.

RUTH 1 – 4

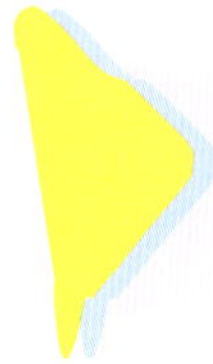

Do you know any babies?

Dear Lord,
Thank You for my grandparents.
They always have time to read to me
or play games.
They like to tickle and play and
laugh.
And they like ice cream and going to
the park, too.
Mostly though, God, they love me.
Please take care of them, Lord.
I think they must be a lot like You.

Anonymous

David and the Giant

David was a young, Israelite shepherd. Goliath was a big Philistine soldier. He was three metres tall! Their countries were enemies.

One day David and Goliath had a fight. Goliath wore armour and had a big spear. David only had his slingshot and five stones. But God helped young David win the battle that day.

1 SAMUEL 17:4–50

Point to David's slingshot.

The Lord is good to me,
  and so I thank the Lord.
For giving me the things I need:
  the sun, the rain, and the
  apple seed!
The Lord is good to me.

Traditional

King David

God chose David to become king. All of God's people met at Hebron. There they made an agreement with David. Then the people poured oil on David's head to make him their king.

David was a great king. He ruled God's people for 40 years.

2 SAMUEL 5:1–12

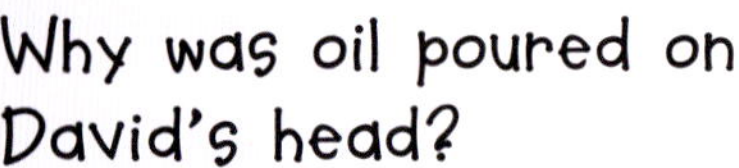

Why was oil poured on David's head?

There is no place where God is not – wherever I go, God is. Now and always he upholds me with his power and keeps me safe in his love.

Unknown

Solomon Is Wise

When David died, his son Solomon became king. God said, "Solomon, ask for anything you want. I will give it to you." Solomon asked God for wisdom to rule God's people well. God was happy Solomon had asked for wisdom instead of money. So, He made Solomon the wisest and richest man who has ever lived.

1 KINGS 3:4–15

Who is the wisest man God made?

Dear Lord,

Thank You that I am sometimes
strong,
help me when I am still weak;
Thank You that I am sometimes wise,
help me when I am still foolish;
Thank You that sometimes I have
done well,
forgive me the times I have failed
You;
And teach me to serve You and Your
world
with love and faith and truth,
with hope and grace and good
humour. Amen.

A Swaledale Parish Prayer

Brave Queen Esther

Haman hated God's people, the Jews. He tricked King Xerxes into making a law to kill all the Jews. Esther was the queen, and King Xerxes loved her. But Esther was a Jew. She bravely told the king about Haman's trick. The king became angry and had Haman killed. Brave Esther had saved God's people.

ESTHER 2 – 9

Point to Esther's crown.

Dear God,

When people shout in anger help me
to speak calmly.
When people threaten to hit me and
hurt me keep me from striking back.
When people try to lead me into a
world of wrong doing give me the
strength to walk away and a safe
place to go.

Sophie Piper

My Shepherd

The Lord is like a kind shepherd. And we are like His sheep. He gives us everything we need. He gives us a nice place to sleep, cool water to drink, and good food to eat. He

protects us from our enemies. We don't need to be afraid because He is always with us and we can live with Him forever.

PSALM 23

Who helps us when we are afraid?

May the road rise to meet you,
May the wind be always at your
back,
May the sun shine warm on your
face,
The rain fall softly on your fields;
And until we meet again,
May God hold you in the palm of
His hand.

Traditional, Irish

Shadrach, Meshach, and Abednego

Shadrach, Meshach, and Abednego loved God. The king of Babylon built an idol for his people to worship. But these men would not worship the idol. So, the king put them in a hot fire. God sent His angel to save them from the fire. The king was amazed and began to worship God, too.

DANIEL 3:1–29

Who saved the men in the fire?

Oh God, You are my God,
And I will ever praise You.
I will seek You in the morning,
And I will learn to walk in Your
ways.
And step by step You'll lead me,
And I will follow You all of my
days.

Rich Mullins

Daniel and the Lions

King Darius made a law for people not to pray to God. But Daniel kept praying to God three times a day. So, the king threw Daniel in a den of lions. God loved Daniel and kept the lions from hurting him. The king was surprised to find Daniel alive. Then King Darius believed in God, too.

DANIEL 6:1–23

Where is the lion?

God be in my head
And in my understanding.
God be in mine eyes
And in my looking.
God be in my mouth
And in my speaking.
God be in my heart
And in my thinking.

Unknown

Jonah and the Big Fish

God told Jonah to go to Nineveh to preach. But Jonah ran away on a boat. So, God sent a big storm. The men in the boat knew the storm was Jonah's fault. Jonah had not obeyed God. So, they threw Jonah into the sea. Then God sent a big fish to swallow Jonah. After three days, God made the fish spit Jonah onto dry land. Then Jonah went to Nineveh.

JONAH 1 – 3

How long was Jonah inside the fish?

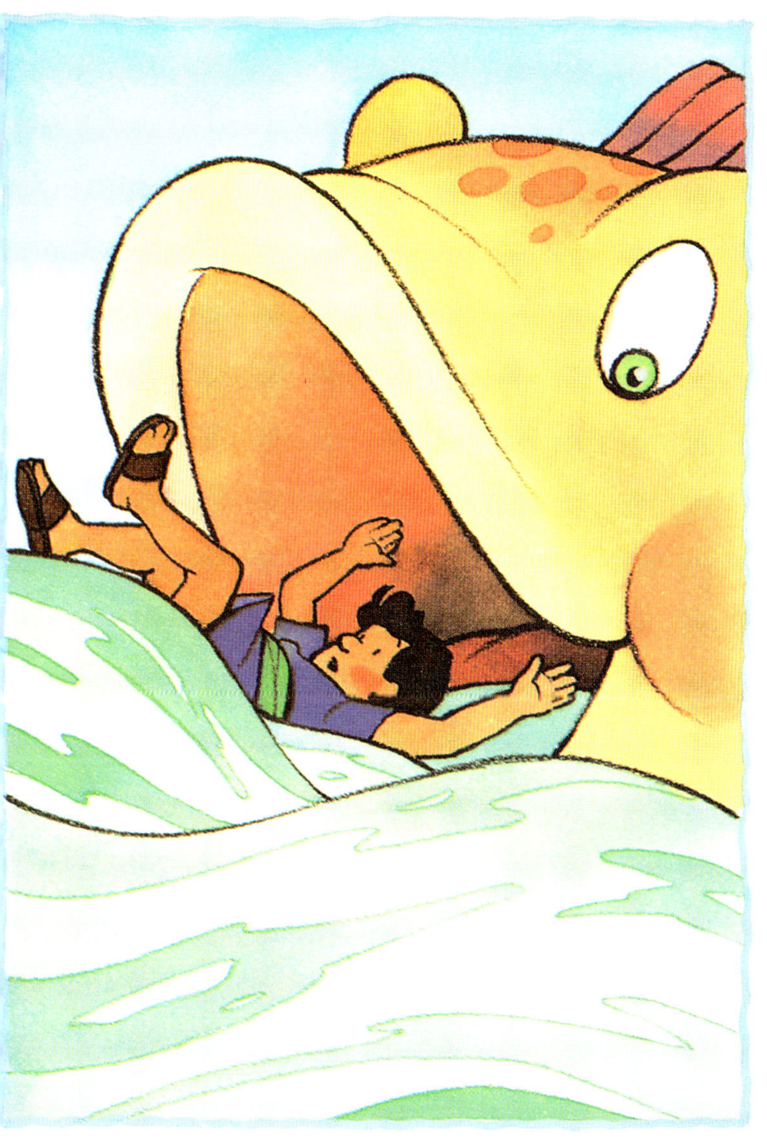

Please give me what I ask,
dear Lord,
If You'd be glad about it.
But if You think it's not for me,
Please help me do without it.

Traditional

NEW TESTAMENT

STORIES

John Is Born

God's angel told Zechariah that his wife, Elizabeth, would have a baby. The angel told Zechariah to name the baby John. Zechariah didn't believe the angel. So God wouldn't let him talk until the baby was born. When the baby came, the people asked Zechariah to name him. He wrote, "His name is John." Then Zechariah could talk again.

LUKE 1:5–20, 57–66

What was the baby's name?

His
name is
JOHN

God has blessed me, God has made me happy.
Our God is coming to help us.
God's promises are all coming true.
Dear God you give good things to those who honour you.

Mary Joslin

Jesus Is Born

An angel from God told Mary she would have a baby boy. The baby would be God's only Son. The angel told Mary to name the baby Jesus. He said the baby would grow up to save people from their sins. Later, the baby was born in a stable in Bethlehem. His bed was a box where animals are fed.

LUKE 1:26–33, 2:1–7

Where was Jesus born?

Christmas

Away in a manger, no crib for a bed,
The little Lord Jesus laid down
  His sweet head;
The stars in the sky looked
  down where He lay,
The little Lord Jesus, asleep on
  the hay.
Be near me, Lord Jesus; I ask
  Thee to stay
Close by me for ever, and love me,
  I pray;
Bless all the dear children in
  Thy tender care,
Prepare us for heaven, to live
  with Thee there.

Martin Luther

The Shepherds

The night Jesus was born, some shepherds were in the field with their sheep. Suddenly, they saw an angel. And they were afraid. The angel told them not to be afraid. He was bringing good news. He said Jesus the Saviour had been born. The shepherds were happy. And they went to worship Jesus.

LUKE 2:8–20

What was the angel's good news?

Christmas

What can I give Him,
Poor as I am?
If I were a shepherd,
I would bring Him a lamb.
If I were a wise man,
I would do my part.
But what can I give Him?
Give Him my heart.

Christina G. Rossetti

The Wise Men

Some wise men from the East saw a bright new star. They knew the star was for God's Son. And they wanted to worship Him. So, they followed the star until they found baby Jesus. They gave baby Jesus some very special gifts.

MATTHEW 2:1–12

Point to the star.

My Birthday

Dear Lord, I am happy today
because it is MY BIRTHDAY!
I was born on a day like today.
It was a great day for my family,
one they could never forget.
Thank You for fun things,
like cake and candles,
for family and friends and
presents and birthday cards.
But most of all, Lord, thank You
for giving me life!

Sheryl Crawford

The Boy Jesus

Jesus went to Jerusalem with His parents. He was 12 years old. After His parents had started home, they couldn't find Jesus. So, they went back to Jerusalem to look for Him. They looked for three days. Finally, they found Him in the temple talking to the teachers about God.

LUKE 2:41–52

Where did Jesus' parents find Him?

Lord, keep us safe this night,
Secure from all our fears.
May angels guard us while we sleep,
Till morning light appears.

Traditional

Jesus Feeds 5,000 People

More than 5,000 people followed Jesus far from town. Jesus taught them and healed the sick. In the afternoon, Jesus' followers wanted to send the people away to find food. But Jesus told them to feed the people themselves. The followers only had five small loaves of bread and two fish.

So, Jesus took the food, thanked God for it, and fed all 5,000 people.

MATTHEW 14:13–21

What did Jesus feed the people?

Thank you for the world so sweet,
Thank you for the food we eat,
Thank you for the birds that sing,
Thank you, God, for everything!

E. Rutter Leatham

Jesus Stops a Storm

Jesus and His followers were in a boat during a bad storm. Jesus was asleep, and His followers were very scared. They thought Jesus didn't care if they drowned. So, they woke Him up.

Jesus told the storm to be quiet. Then the wind stopped, and the lake became calm. And the followers were amazed at His power!

MARK 4:35–41

Are you ever afraid during a storm?

Dear God, be good to me.
The sea is so wide,
and my boat is so small.

The Breton Fisherman's Prayer

Jesus and the Children

People brought their children to see Jesus. His followers tried to send the children away. But Jesus told them to let the children come to Him. He told his followers to love God like the little children do.

Then Jesus took the children in his arms and blessed them.

MARK 10:13–16

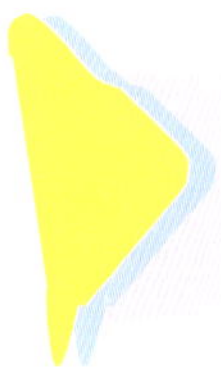

Do you think Jesus loves children?

All for You, dear
  God.
Everything I do,
Or think,
Or say,
The whole day long.
Help me to be good.

Unknown

Jesus and the Blind Man

Bartimaeus was blind. He was sitting beside the road. Then he heard Jesus coming. He called out for Jesus to help him. Jesus said, "Bartimaeus, what do you want me to do?" Bartimaeus said he wanted to see again. Jesus healed Bartimaeus so he could see. Then Bartimaeus followed Jesus.

MARK 10:46–52

What would it be like to be blind?

I feel happy, Jesus!
I am happy when I laugh with
friends, or hold a puppy.
I feel happy eating ice cream, or
listening to a story.
I feel happy when someone says,
"I love you."
Lord, I am happy because I belong
to You!
That is the best thing of all to be
happy about!

Sheryl Crawford

The Wasteful Son

Once the younger of two brothers took his part of their father's money. He went to a faraway country. There he spent all his money. He was poor. He had no food to eat. He took a job feeding pigs. Then he decided to go home. He was sorry for acting so badly.

His father was so happy his son had come home, he gave a party.

LUKE 15:11–32

It is not good to run away from home.

God, we thank you for this food,
For rest and home and all things
good;
For wind and rain and sun above,
But most of all for those we love.

Maryleona Frost

Zacchaeus Meets Jesus

Zacchaeus cheated people by making them pay too much tax. One day Jesus came to town. Zacchaeus was too short to see over the people. So, he climbed into a tree to see Jesus. Jesus saw him and told him to come down. Then Jesus went home with Zacchaeus for dinner. And Zacchaeus never cheated people again.

LUKE 19:1–10

How was Zacchaeus able to see Jesus?

Father, we thank You for the night,
And for the pleasant morning light,
For rest and food and loving care,
And all that makes the day so fair.

Help us to do the things we should,
To be to others kind and good;
In all we do and all we say,
To grow more loving every day.

Unknown

Lazarus Lives Again!

Jesus' friend Lazarus died. So, Jesus went to where Lazarus was buried. And Jesus cried. Then Jesus did a wonderful thing! He called out to Lazarus in his grave. He said, "Lazarus, come out!"

Then Lazarus came walking out of the grave. He was alive again! Jesus had raised him from death.

JOHN 11:1–44

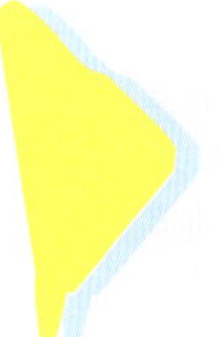

Was Jesus sad when his friend died?

Now I lay me down to sleep.
I pray Thee, Lord, my soul to keep.
Your love be with me through
  the night
And wake me with the morning
  light.

Traditional

Jesus' Last Supper

The last supper Jesus shared with His followers was called Passover. He held some bread. He said the bread was like His body. Then He held a cup of wine. He said the wine was like His blood. He asked them to remember Him with wine and bread until He comes back.

LUKE 22:14–20

Does Jesus want us to remember Him?

God is great.
God is good.
Let us thank Him
for our food.

Traditional

Good News

God's Son, Jesus, was killed on a cross by His enemies. It was a dark, sad day. Jesus' friends took Him down from the cross. They wrapped Him in special cloths and buried Him. But three days later Jesus came back to life!

Jesus is more powerful than death. That is why Jesus can save us from our sins. And that is good news!

JOHN 19:16 – 20:18

What is the good news?

Easter

He is Lord,
He is Lord!
He is risen from the dead
  and He is Lord!
Every knee shall bow;
Every tongue confess,
that Jesus Christ is Lord.

Traditional

Jesus Goes Back to Heaven

Jesus' work on earth was done. He told His followers to tell the whole world the good news about Him. Then Jesus disappeared into a cloud. He went back to heaven.

His followers were still looking into the sky when two men appeared. They told Jesus' followers that Jesus would come back to earth some day.

ACTS 1:6–11

Where is Jesus now?

Dear God, my friend is moving,
and I'm so sad.
We've had so much fun together,
and I don't want her to move.
Please help her to find new
friends where she's going so
she won't be lonely.
And help me to make new
friends, too.
Thank You, Jesus, for being my
best friend.

Anonymous

Jesus' Followers Share

Jesus' followers shared everything they had. Each person had what he needed to live. The followers gave

money, food, and clothes to those who needed it. And God blessed all the followers very much.

ACTS 4:32–35

What can you share?

God bless all those that I love.
God bless all those that love me.
God bless all those that love
those that I love, and all those
that love those who love me.

New England Sampler

Saul Meets Jesus

Saul was going to Damascus to hurt Jesus' followers. On the way, a bright light blinded Saul. Then Jesus' voice said, "Saul, I am Jesus. Go to Damascus and wait. Someone will come to tell you what you must do." Three days later, Ananias taught Saul to follow Jesus.

ACTS 9:1–19

What did Jesus tell Saul?

TO
DAMASCUS

A great grey elephant,
A little yellow bee,
A tiny purple violet,
A tall green tree,
A red and white sailboat
On a blue sea –
All these things
You gave to me,
When you made
My eyes to see –
Thank You, God.

National Society for the
Prevention of Blindness, Inc.

Peter and the Angel

Peter was in jail. He was sleeping between two soldiers. They had chains on Peter. Soldiers guarded the jail door, too. Suddenly, an angel came. Peter's chains fell off. And the angel led Peter out of the jail. Peter escaped! God saved Peter from his enemies.

ACTS 12:6–10

Who helped Peter escape from jail?

Zzz
Zzz
Zzz

Day by day, dear Lord, of Thee
Three things I pray:
To see Thee more clearly,
Love Thee more dearly,
Follow Thee more nearly,
Day by day.

St. Richard of Chichester

Jesus Will Come Back!

Someday Jesus will come back from heaven. He said, "I am coming soon!" When He comes, He will bring rewards with Him. He will give gifts to those who do good.

Those who believe in Jesus will go to heaven with Him.

REVELATION 22:12–14, 20–21

Will you be glad to see Jesus?

Jesus, someone I care for lives
with You now.
I feel very sad because that person
is not here.
Sometimes I cry... to let the
sadness out.
Lord, You say that people who
live with You are happy.
In heaven, there are angels and
friends and family.
Jesus, please help me to remember
that someday we will be together
again with the ones we love...
And we will live forever with
You in heaven!

Sheryl Crawford

Published in the UK in 2010 by Candle Books
(a publishing imprint of Lion Hudson plc).

Distributed by Marston Book Services Ltd,
PO Box 269, Abingdon, Oxon OX14 4YN

The publisher has made every effort to locate the owners of all copyrighted material and to obtain permission to reprint the prayers in this book. Any errors are unintentional, and corrections will be made in future editions if necessary. The publishers acknowledge special thanks for the permission received from the following:

Celebration for "The Butterfly Song" by Brian Howard, copyright © 1974, 1975 by Celebration. "A Great Grey Elephant" courtesy of the National Society to Prevent Blindness. "Sometimes by Step" by Rich Mullins, copyright © 1992 BMG Songs, Inc./Kid Brothers of St. Frank Publishing.

Co-edition organised and produced by
Lion Hudson plc, Wilkinson House,
Jordan Hill Road, Oxford OX2 8DR
Tel: +44 (0)1865 302750
Fax: +44 (0)1865 302757
Email: coed@lionhudson.com
www.lionhudson.com

ISBN 978 1 85985 819 6

Printed in China